The BOYS' BOOK of SURVIVAL

HOW TO SURVIVE ANYTHING, ANYWHERE

Written by Guy Campbell
Illustrated by Simon Ecob
Edited by Rachel Carter
Designed by Zoe Quayle
With thanks to Toby Buchan
and Philippa Wingate

The Boys' Book of Survival

HOW TO SURVIVE ANYTHING, ANYWHERE

SCHOLASTIC INC.

New York   Toronto   London   Auckland
Sydney   Mexico City   New Delhi   Hong Kong

Library of Congress Cataloging-in-Publication Data

Campbell, Guy.
The boys' book of survival : how to survive anything, anywhere / written by Guy Campbell ; illustrated by Simon Ecob. — 1st American ed.
p. cm.
ISBN-13: 978-0-545-08536-6
ISBN-10: 0-545-08536-5
1. Camping — Juvenile literature. 2. Boys — Recreation — Juvenile literature. I. Ecob, Simon. II. Title.
GV191.7.C3475 2009
796.54 — dc22
2008019893

First published in Great Britain in 2008 by Buster Books, an imprint of Michael O'Mara Books Limited, 9 Lion Yard, Tremadoc Road, London SW4 7NQ, United Kingdom.

Text and illustrations copyright © Buster Books 2008

Cover design by Angie Allison
(from an original design by www.blacksheep-uk.com)
Cover illustration by Paul Moran

All rights reserved. Published by Scholastic Inc., 557 Broadway, New York, NY 10012. SCHOLASTIC and associated logos are trademarks and/or registered trademarks of Scholastic Inc.

15   16   17   15   16   17/0

Printed in the U.S.A.   23
First American edition, January 2009

WARNING

The survival techniques in this book are for use only in emergencies. Take a responsible adult with you if you go on an expedition, because it is never a good idea to undertake any of the activities described here by yourself.

We urge you at all times to make yourself aware of and obey all laws and regulations and respect all rights, including the rights of landowners, and all relevant laws protecting animals and plants and controlling the carrying and use of implements such as catapults and knives.

DISCLAIMER

The publisher and the author disclaim all liability for accidents or injuries or loss of any nature that may occur as a result of the use or misuse of the information and guidance given in this book.

Above all, exercise common sense, particularly when fire or sharp objects are involved, and follow safety precautions and advice from responsible adults at all times. That said, it is fun to learn new skills, and they may one day be useful.

CONTENTS

HOW TO PLAN A GROUP EXPEDITION

Expedition is the word used to describe a trip with a purpose. Here are some tips on how to make sure any expedition you and your team embark upon is well planned and goes without a hitch:

1. The first thing to do when planning an expedition is to come up with a mission statement. This is a couple of sentences that clearly describe where you are going on the trip, why you are going, and what you want to achieve.

Here is a sample mission statement:
"I plan to lead my team through the Atlas Mountains in Morocco. We will observe the hill tribes living there, and take some fantastic photos of the people and the landscape."

2. Use a map to plan your route to and from your destination. Work out how far your team will travel each day and plan where you will camp each night. Plan at least one alternative route both there and back in case you come across any obstacles on your journey.

3. Study books about previous expeditions to the area. Read and compare the accounts of at least three different people. Then make notes on the following points:

a) Decide on a start date and an end date for your expedition. Investigate the type of weather you can expect in the area at that time of year, as this will affect the clothing and camping equipment you will need to take.

b) What type of ground will you be covering? Is the terrain flat or mountainous? Do you need to take ropes and climbing gear, or would it be wiser to take cross-country skis?

c) Are there any natural sources of food or water along your planned route? How many days will you need to travel before you reach them? This will affect your calculations of how many days' food and drink rations you need to carry at the beginning of your journey.

d) Are there any deadly creatures you should watch out for along the way, such as snakes or poisonous spiders? This will influence the medical supplies you pack.

4. Make a list of everything that could go wrong on the expedition. What if someone gets sick from food poisoning or breaks a leg? Make a list of the supplies and equipment you'll need to deal with each situation.

5. Assign each member of your team an essential duty. These duties might include map reading, shelter building, monitoring rations, fetching water, cooking, gathering wood and building fires, keeping the camp clean, and watching out for dangerous animals.

6. Use all the information you have gathered to write up a trip plan. Give a copy of the plan to everyone who will be going on the expedition. Leave a copy with someone who is not. This person can alert the authorities if you don't return on time.

HOW TO MAKE YOUR OWN SURVIVAL PACK

The equipment you take with you will depend on the type of expedition you are planning. But whether you're camping in the wilderness, hiking through mountains, or trekking through jungles, there are some expedition essentials that will keep you warm, dry, and well fed:

ESSENTIAL ITEMS

• Water (as much as you can carry) • Water-purifying tablets • Food rations (including high-energy food, such as chocolate, energy bars, and nuts) • Maps • A good compass • Warm clothing (including a hat and gloves) • Hiking boots • A waterproof coat • Camping equipment: tent, sleeping bag, cooking utensils • A first-aid kit • A whistle • A flashlight (with spare bulb and batteries) • A pocketknife • A waterproof sheet (5 feet x 7 feet)

• Wristwatch • Sturdy plastic bags for carrying water
• Fish hooks and twine • Fully charged cell phone
• Waterproof matches, a lighter, and tinder • Magnifying
glass (which can be used to start a fire) • A candle • At
least 25 feet of cord or rope • Wire for making snares
• Insect repellent • Sunscreen • Emergency blanket

BEFORE YOU LEAVE

• Check that all your electrical appliances are working and
fully charged, or have new batteries before you set off.

• Take a bivouac sack (also called a survival bag or bivi
bag) with you. This is a large, lightweight, brightly colored
waterproof bag that you can sleep in if necessary in an
emergency.

• Even if your expedition should only take you a couple of
hours, pack the equipment and rations you would need to
survive for at least twenty-four hours in an emergency.

HOW TO BE A GOOD LEADER

There may be a time when you find yourself with a group of people in a potentially dangerous situation. Someone needs to take the lead — and that someone could be you. Here are some things to remember if you step forward to take the role of leader.

MAKE A STRONG START

When you first meet the members of your team, make eye contact with each of them. This gives an excellent first impression. A confident, firm (but not too firm) handshake helps, too. Stand upright with your shoulders back. This will give your teammates confidence in your abilities. If you slouch, you will look uninterested and nervous, which are not leadership qualities.

Try really hard to remember everyone's name and repeat it as you introduce yourself: "Hello, Jack. I'm James." This will make people feel you're interested in them and they will be more likely to trust you.

BE GOOD AT SOMETHING

People often admire someone who is good at something. If you read this book from cover to cover, your excellent survival knowledge will be sure to impress your team. Being good at sports is impressive, but if you lack athletic skills don't worry, metalworking and woodworking talent can be really useful in survival situations. Failing that, make sure you have the right equipment for an expedition. Being the owner of the biggest and the best tools is always a plus.

If all else fails, be witty and charming. Many leaders get to the top by putting people at ease and making them laugh.

ALWAYS TRY TO REMAIN POSITIVE

• When in a difficult situation, try to see solutions to the problems that face you rather than moaning about them. Complaining wastes time and can lower your team's spirits. Try to keep your worries and anxieties to yourself.

• Keep any criticism to a minimum. Let's face it – nobody's perfect. If you are slow to blame people when things go wrong and quick to praise them if they perform a task well, your teammates will stay enthusiastic and cooperative.

• Don't ask anyone to perform any chores or take any risks that you wouldn't be happy to take on yourself.

• When one of your team members is speaking to you, pay careful attention to what he or she is saying. Being aware of and making use of your team members' various talents and expertise can only get you ahead.

• Don't play favorites. Make sure everyone feels that he or she is a valued member of the team.

HOW TO AVOID PIRANHAS

If you find yourself on an expedition in a South American rain forest and you have no choice but to cross a river, take a moment to think about piranhas. These ferocious fish have razor-sharp teeth and a frightening reputation for stripping the flesh off animals. Piranhas are not ideal swimming companions.

PIRANHA POINTERS

• In general, piranhas prefer to eat dead animal carcasses over healthy, live humans. Still, it's best not to enter piranha-infested waters if you have an open cut or sore that is bleeding.

• Piranhas live in warm waters that are still or flow slowly. Make sure the point at which you attempt to cross the river is one where the water is cold or fast moving.

• Wait until dark before attempting to cross, as this is when piranhas are least active. Then swim or wade smoothly through the water, keeping any splashing to a minimum so as not to alert the piranhas to your presence.

DON'T PANIC

Piranhas don't go out of their way to attack humans unless they are really hungry. They are most dangerous during dry seasons, when water levels are low and food is hard to come by. So if it's dry season, you might want to set up camp and wait until another time of year to cross that river!

HOW TO SURVIVE A TORNADO

Tornadoes (also known as twisters) are windstorms that create a highly destructive, whirling funnel of air. They cause devastating damage to the areas they hit and happen very quickly and with little warning.

PREPARATION

The best way to survive a tornado is to be prepared for it. If you live in an area that is prone to tornadoes, keep an

eye on the weather by regularly logging onto a weather Web site, or by tuning into TV or radio weather forecasts.

Keep a tornado kit in a metal box inside your house. The kit should include a fully charged cell phone, a portable radio, first-aid supplies, a bell, horn, or whistle for signaling, and a flashlight.

Additional supplies should include food, water, batteries, and protective clothing. Keep your tornado kit somewhere handy so you can grab it easily if a twister hits.

EARLY WARNING SIGNS

Here are some signs that indicate a twister may be heading your way:

• Often you will hear a tornado coming before you see it. Listen for a sound like a waterfall that turns into a roar as it gets closer. The sound of a tornado has been compared to that of a train or even a jet engine.

• The sky often turns a sickly green or greenish-black color just before a tornado hits.

• It may suddenly start to hail.

• You may notice clouds that are moving very fast and possibly twisting into a cone shape.

• You might see debris, such as dust, branches, and leaves dropping from the sky.

When the tornado arrives, you can expect to see a funnel-shaped cloud that is spinning rapidly. Debris will be pulled upward into the funnel.

GET INSIDE

The best place to be when a tornado arrives is inside. Houses in areas that are prone to tornadoes often have storm cellars underneath them. These are the safest places to hide. If the building you're in does not have a cellar, head for the lowest floor. Find the smallest room on that floor, such as a bathroom or closet. If that's not possible, look for a room in the middle of the house with no windows. A hallway may provide the best shelter.

Close any doors and windows that are located on the same side of the room as the approaching tornado. Open all the doors and windows on the other side of the room. This will help prevent the powerful wind from entering the building. Tornadoes have been known to pick up entire structures.

Take shelter under some solid furniture, such as a heavy kitchen table. If you are in a bathroom, jump into the bathtub. Cover yourself with a mattress, a sofa, pillows, towels, or anything soft that you can get your hands on to protect yourself from flying debris.

SURVIVING OUTSIDE

If you are unlucky enough to be caught outside without buildings nearby, try to get out of the path of the tornado by moving to the side, rather than by trying to outrun it.

Never hide behind a tree or climb into a car, truck, or tractor, as these may be sucked up by the tornado.

If the only shelter you can find is in a ditch, lie face down and use your arms to protect your head and neck.

HOW TO CHOOSE A GOOD PLACE TO SPEND THE NIGHT IN THE WILDERNESS

If you find yourself stranded in an unfamiliar environment, your top priority is to find a safe place to sleep well before darkness falls.

TAKE COVER

The most important thing a shelter provides is protection from the elements. In desert areas, you will need to stay out of the sun. In mountainous or in polar regions, rain, snow, and wind will seriously threaten your chances of survival.

Caves provide good natural shelter. Always check them out carefully first – you don't want to find you are sharing your newfound home with a surprised wild animal, such

as a hibernating bear or a mountain lion. Scout around for telltale signs that the cave may be occupied. These include bones, nests, or droppings inside or near the cave entrance, and clumps of vegetation that are being used as bedding.

If you can't find a cave, look for a spot that is shielded from the elements. Camping at the base of a rockface or cliff will offer some shelter. However, check that there aren't any loose rocks lying around, as these would suggest you are in danger from falling debris.

THE IDEAL SPOT

A clearing in the woods is the ideal spot to make camp, especially if there is a fast-running stream nearby. That way you will have building materials for your shelter, wood for your fire, and water for drinking, washing, and cooking.

PLACES TO AVOID

When looking for a place to set up camp, here are some places to avoid:

• Stay away from areas close to ponds or lakes. Water that isn't flowing attracts insects that might bite or sting you.

• Don't camp at the bottom of a hill. Rainwater may run down the hillside and flood your shelter.

• Never camp at the top of a hill, as you will be exposed to the wind and rain, and your shelter could easily be blown away.

• Avoid camping beside a cliff or rockface in snowy terrain, as this is where snow may build up and could bury you while you sleep. There might also be a danger of avalanches.

HOW TO SURVIVE FALLING OFF A HORSE

Horses have a habit of not doing quite what you want, and this occasionally includes dumping you on the ground. You are more likely to survive in one piece if you learn how to take a fall.

1. Never mount your trusty steed without the right safety gear. A riding helmet could save your life. Wearing jeans and a tough, long-sleeve jacket will protect your arms and legs from being scratched by low branches or being grazed if you fall on rough ground.

2. Once you realize your horse is impossible to control and that falling off is inevitable, try to look for a soft patch of ground to land on. It's better to fall off sooner onto sand, soil, or grass rather than later onto rocks or gravel.

3. As you begin to fall, it is important to accept that you and your horse are going to part company for a while. Don't hang on for dear life. Kick your feet out of the stirrups and drop the reins to ensure that you aren't dragged cross-country for miles.

4. As you fall, try not to tense up. Keep your limbs as loose as possible. Resist the temptation to throw your arms straight out in front of you to break your fall. The only thing you will break is your bones. The more relaxed your body is, the better your landing will be.

5. As you fall, try to propel yourself as far away from your horse as you can to avoid being trampled under its hooves.

6. Ideally, you should attempt to land on your feet, bending your knees immediately on impact. Then curl into a ball to protect your vital organs and roll away from your horse. Cover your head and neck with your arms to protect your head.

7. Don't jump up as soon as you have rolled to a stop. One by one, test your fingers, arms, legs, and especially your neck for damage by gently moving them. If everything seems intact, get up very slowly. If you are injured, any quick movements could make matters worse.

The good news is that you are in one piece. The bad news is that your horse is a mile away — and it probably won't be the last time you take a fall.

HOW TO SURVIVE A DUEL

Imagine you wake up on a Monday morning and instead of opening your eyes and seeing your messy bedroom, you find yourself transported back in time to the seventeenth century. Superb sword-fighting skills would be essential to your survival.

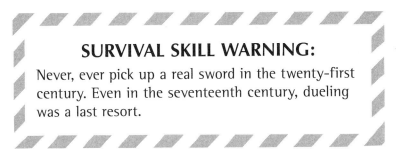

SURVIVAL SKILL WARNING:

Never, ever pick up a real sword in the twenty-first century. Even in the seventeenth century, dueling was a last resort.

TOOLS OF THE TRADE

If you are right-handed, hold your sword in your right hand and vice versa if you are left-handed. Your sword is thin and whippy, so you shouldn't need to hold it with both hands.

THE *EN GARDE* POSITION

Every musketeer knows the foundation of all good sword-fighting moves is a steady *en garde* position. *En garde* allows fighters to switch quickly between defending themselves or attacking their opponents.

Here's how it is done:

1. Stand one large step away from being able to touch your opponent's outstretched sword. Any closer and

you will be left standing in your enemy's strike range if your strike misses. Make sure your back is to the sun — that way your enemy's body will be well lit, but yours will be hidden in shadow.

2. Turn your body to the side. Right-handers: Point your right foot directly toward the opponent, keeping your left foot where it is (left-handers vice versa).

3. Bend your knees so that your body is well balanced.

4. Keeping your back as straight as possible, bend your sword arm at the elbow. Hold the handle (called the grip) of your sword level with your hips, with the point level with your head but slanting away from your body and toward your enemy. This stance will ensure your body is protected from your head to your hips.

5. Hold your other hand behind your back or to one side, so it doesn't get in your way. You should feel well balanced and comfortable in this position.

TACTICS

As your opponent attempts to strike, straighten your arm and go in for the attack. Try to knock aside his or her sword with your own blade. Then quickly step forward and counter his or her strike with your own. Any strike is a good strike. Your opponent's legs, arms, and even his or her hands are often easier to target than his or her torso.

When fighting, conserve energy by keeping your movements to a minimum. Let your opponent do all the running around. He or she will soon tire. If you can, back your opponent into furniture and make him or her fall over. When your opponent is on the ground and swordless, you can afford to be chivalrous and let him or her get up unharmed.

HOW TO SURVIVE AN ALIEN INVASION

No one is really sure what aliens look like. However, many people believe that they do exist, and one day you might come face-to-face with one. If you meet an alien, whether it is a little green man, a tall purple woman, or a shapeless blob of talking mucus, be very careful. It may be a tourist alien, here on Earth for two weeks to see the sights and soak up some of our oxygen-rich atmosphere. However, it could be scouting for a forthcoming alien invasion.

JUST VISITING

If you're lucky enough to have bumped into an alien tourist, this is a great opportunity to make a new friend. Be as charming as possible, no matter how revolting it looks, and it may invite you to its home planet in return. Show it the sights. Point out that Earth only has one sun, that it has one moon orbiting it, and that our sky is blue. Some planets have many moons and different-colored skies, so be prepared for the alien to find this quite odd.

Be hospitable. You don't want the alien returning home to its planet and telling terrible stories about how horrible earthlings are. Then the alien may come back with all its friends and family to either take over or destroy the earth.

WORLD DOMINATION

Of course, if this alien is planning to take over the world, it will not have much time for chitchat. It will probably say something like: "Bow down, inferior earthling. You

stand before the Emperor Zog. Prepare to meet your doom."
In this case, run like the wind and alert the authorities so
they can impose a state of national emergency. If, however,
your path is blocked by the spacecraft parked on your
doorstep, try holding up a mirror in front of your
extraterrestrial visitor. It will never have seen its reflection,
so this is guaranteed to baffle it completely and keep it
busy until help arrives.

SURVIVE THE INVASION

Aliens usually start their invasions in capital cities because
lots of powerful people work there. Gather together your
friends and family and head away from the cities as soon
as you hear of the invasion. Besides, fighting an alien
invasion is best left to the professionals.

27

Take a radio with you so you can keep up to date with the latest alien movements and listen for the all-clear. Choose a place to hide that is as remote as possible so that you can stay out of the invaders' way.

All you need to do now is wait for Earth's armed forces to win the day, or for the aliens to get tired of the earth's weather patterns and go home. Aliens do not like the rain and will do their utmost to avoid a shower. A few good thunderstorms should send them packing.

Survival Tip: Aliens might try to pose as humans, so look out for unusual behavior in your loved ones. Avoid people with glowing eyes or weird-sounding voices. Anyone showing confusion when performing simple human tasks such as opening doors and putting on clothes is also a dead giveaway.

HOW TO SURVIVE A BULLY

Unfortunately, bullies crop up in many different places, from playgrounds to street corners. Some people just seem to like to tease and scare others to make themselves feel stronger and more important. Here are some tips to help you if you are unlucky enough to come across a bully.

DON'T SUFFER IN SILENCE

Being bullied is a really miserable experience, so don't just grin and bear it. Tell someone in a position of authority, such as a teacher or parent, exactly what is happening and let him or her deal with the bully.

Write down exactly what the bully says or does, and make a note of any witnesses to the bullying. That way, you can give an adult an accurate account of what happened.

A bully will seek out victims who appear insecure or scared. Some people find that taking martial arts or self-defense classes helps them feel more confident. However, never use violence against bullies. Beating a bully up might seem like an attractive option, but in reality it will only make things worse. Leave his or her punishment to an adult.

Try not to show the bully you are intimidated or hurt by his or her behavior. Counter his or her jeering and taunting with a smile. Don't attempt sarcasm or jokes at the bully's expense, however. That will just give him or her more reason to continue harassing you. Often a bully who doesn't get a reaction will get bored and leave you alone.

HOW TO SURVIVE A SHARK ATTACK

Unsurprisingly, the best way to survive a shark attack is to avoid sharks in the first place. While the danger of being attacked by a shark is hugely exaggerated in many movies, swimming in shark-infested water isn't a smart thing to do. However, if you do find yourself among fishy friends, take these precautions to minimize your chances of becoming a shark snack:

DOS AND DON'TS

• Sharks like to eat fish. Stay away from fishing boats and groups of seabirds, which is where sharks are likely to be hunting.

• If you cut yourself, get out of the water immediately. Sharks can smell blood from a long way off and will soon come to investigate the cause of the delicious smell.

• Swim with a group of people. Sharks are less likely to attack if they are outnumbered. Also, you'll be safer with more people keeping an eye out for sharks.

• Wear dark, plain colors. Brightly colored bathing suits or wetsuits and even shiny watches and jewelry may catch the light and make you look like a tasty exotic fish.

• Never provoke a shark by lunging at it or waving your arms and legs around. If a shark feels threatened, it is much more likely to attack.

• Avoid swimming at dusk or in the evening, as this is when sharks are most active. Avoid swimming in deep water, near river mouths, and in murky, frothy water.

ACTION IF ATTACKED

If a shark has decided to attack, it will begin to dart to and fro, zigzagging and lifting its head. Here's what to do:

• Swim away as quickly as you can and get out of the water. If you can't, stay calm. Don't thrash and splash about – the shark will think that you're injured and an easy kill.

• Try to get into a position where your back is protected by rocks, a reef, or by another swimmer. That way you can concentrate on defending yourself from the front.

• When the shark attacks, don't freeze with fear. Hit it with a sharp object or your fists. Aim your blows at its eyes, gills, or at the end of its nose, which are its most sensitive areas.

HOW TO MAKE A LADDER

Here's a quick and easy way to make a ladder. The type of knot you need to use is called a man-harness hitch. You will need two equal lengths of sturdy rope and several short but tough lengths of a branch.

1. Make a loop in one rope.

2. The bottom of the rope crosses over the loop as shown here.

3. Make a twist in the top of the loop.

4. Take the twist over the bottom of the rope and tuck it through the bottom of your loop.

5. Push a length of branch into the new loop. Tug on the rope so the knot takes shape and is tight.

6. Repeat the knots at intervals on this and the other rope to make a ladder.

Important: Have an adult test your ladder before you use it.

HOW TO AVOID BEING ATTACKED BY A POLAR BEAR

Polar bears rarely attack humans, as they prefer a diet of seals and fish to human flesh. However, they're strong and very curious, so it is best to take precautions to avoid an attack.

POLAR PRECAUTIONS

• Visit the South Pole instead of the North Pole. Polar bears only live in the Arctic Circle, so you'll be out of paws' reach at the South Pole.

• When possible, sleep in concrete buildings. Polar bears have claws that can grow up to 3–4 inches long and can easily destroy a tent. Male bears can weigh as much as half a ton and would flatten a wooden hut with ease.

• Polar bears have an excellent sense of smell. Always keep your camp clean and tidy. The smell of trash will attract hungry bears from miles around.

• Stay away from dead animals you find on the ice. A bear may be nearby looking for an easy meal, and if it sees you, it might prefer fresh meat.

• If you do encounter a polar bear, never turn and run. Stand in front of it holding your coat or a blanket over your head to make yourself look bigger than you are. Wave your arms around and make as much noise as possible. With luck, the bear will decide you are too difficult a meal to bother with, and will head off for a seal snack.

HOW TO SURVIVE A LONG CAR JOURNEY

When you're stuck in the back of the car on the way to visit your relatives, boredom can strike at any time. Make sure you survive the trip.

WHAT NOT TO DO

• Don't kick the back of the seat in front of you over and over again.

• Avoid singing the following song over and over again: *"I know a song that'll get on your nerves, get on your nerves, get on your nerves. I know a song that'll get on your nerves, here's how it goes. . . ." (repeat)*

• Resist asking any of the following questions: *"Are we there yet?" "Is it far now?" "When's breakfast/lunch/ dinner?"*

• Don't try to climb into the front seat from the backseat when the car is moving.

• Don't have a backseat burping contest. However bored you are, it's in your best interests not to distract the driver from the road ahead.

GAME ON

Give these games a try and keep yourself entertained for hours on end.

The License Plate Game: This is a classic car trip game that can be played with any number of people. Simply start with the letter *A* and take turns looking for license plates containing the letters *B, C, D,* and so on. Although it's tempting, don't ask the driver to speed up so you can check out the license plate of the car in front of yours.

Bingo: Prepare a bingo sheet in advance for each person to use. Offer a prize to the first person to spot all the items on his or her sheet. The winner gets to choose the radio station for the next half hour or decide where to stop for snacks next.

HOW TO READ A COMPASS

1. Hold the compass out flat so that the needle can spin around freely.

2. Stand still for a few moments until the north-seeking end of the compass needle (usually marked with red paint) settles in one position. This is magnetic north.

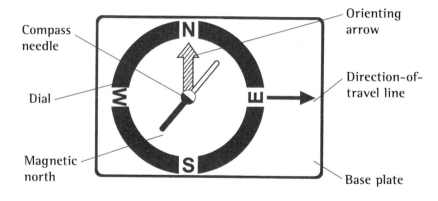

Compass needle

Dial

Magnetic north

Orienting arrow

Direction-of-travel line

Base plate

3. Keep the compass level and turn the dial until the orienting arrow for north is over the colored end of the compass needle. Now you know exactly which way south, east, and west are, too.

Survival Tip: Try not to stand too close to any large metal objects, as these may affect the compass reading. Also, if you happen to have a magnet in your pocket, the needle will point to that rather than finding north, which won't help at all if you are lost.

Once you've learned how to read a compass, you'll be able to use it to find your way even when there are no visible landmarks to take your bearings from. If you are out walking and want to set up camp that evening at the base of a hill in the distance, follow the instructions below:

1. Aim the compass so that the arrow indicating the direction-of-travel is pointing directly at the hill.

2. With the arrow still aimed at the hill, turn the dial until the orienting arrow for north is over the north end of the compass needle.

3. Using these bearings you'll be able to follow the direction-of-travel line toward the hill, even if you have to walk through a forest. Just walk toward the hill, keeping the needle firmly positioned on the mark for north.

HOW TO COPE WITHOUT A COMPASS

If you are unfortunate enough to have forgotten your compass, all is not lost. As long as someone is wearing a wristwatch, you'll be able to use the sun to figure out which way is north.

The sun rises in the east and sets in the west wherever you are. However, at noon in the Northern Hemisphere, the sun is due south and at noon in the Southern Hemisphere, it is due north.

To find south in the Northern Hemisphere, hold your watch horizontally and aim the hour hand directly at the sun. The point on the watch face between twelve o'clock (one o'clock during Daylight Saving Time) and the hour hand is due south.

Northern Hemisphere

To find north in the Southern Hemisphere, aim twelve o'clock on the watch face at the sun and then divide the angle between the hour hand and twelve. This is due north.

Survival Tip: If you have a digital watch, simply draw a clock face on a piece of paper. Look at the time on your digital watch and mark where the hands would be on an analog clock on your picture. Then follow the instructions above.

HOW TO MAKE A COMPASS USING THE SUN

Even without a compass or a watch, it is possible to figure out roughly which direction is north by using the movement of the sun. You'll need a little bit of time to get this right.

You will need:
- A long, straight stick • Two medium-size pebbles
- Some level ground • A piece of string and a twig

1. Place the stick in the ground and mark the tip of the stick's shadow with one pebble in the morning.

2. Draw a semicircular line around the stick (use a piece of string tied to the stick and a twig at the other end to mark the ground). The line should be the same distance away from the stick as the pebble.

3. The stick's shadow will get shorter as the time gets closer to noon, and longer as the afternoon goes on. Wait until the stick's shadow touches the edge of the semicircle again and mark the point with your second pebble.

4. As the sun moves across the sky from east to west, the shadow from the stick will move in the opposite direction, from west to east. The line between your morning pebble and your evening pebble marks a line from west to east, so if you draw another line at a right angle to this, you will also have north and south. (Remember north and south are reversed in the Southern Hemisphere.)

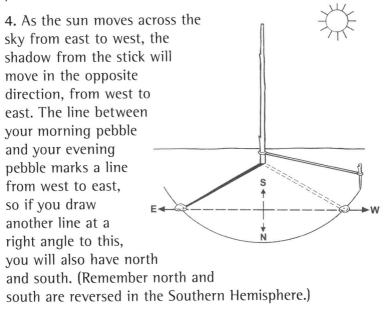

39

HOW TO SURVIVE A HAUNTING

Whether or not you personally believe in ghosts, some people certainly do. They will swear that things happen that are hard to explain – objects move, there are strange noises, there are cold areas in rooms, or they even catch glimpses of the ghosts themselves.

Perhaps you feel fine or even excited about having a ghost in your house. This is useful when surviving a haunting because experts believe that making friends with a ghost is the best way to stop it from doing annoying things around your house.

Begin by talking to the ghost. Some say that ghosts are confused and unsure of why they are stuck on Earth. Try reminding the ghost that it has loved ones waiting for it "on the other side." This might spur it to move on. Or you can try simply telling the ghost in a loud voice that you'd like it to leave. You never know — it might be a timid spirit that is easily spooked.

OUT, OUT, OUT!

If giving the ghost a good talking-to doesn't work, carry a lit candle and a silver bell into every room in the house. Walk to each corner of each room with the candle in one hand and ring the bell with the other.

Next take the candle and the bell outside and visit each corner of the house, too. This supposedly has the effect of chasing the ghost out of any corner it has become comfortable in.

ANTISPOOK DEVICES

Other ways of making the house unfriendly to ghosts include sprinkling a thin line of sea salt along each windowsill and doorway, scattering rice on the kitchen floor overnight, painting your front door red, or placing your shoes on the floor pointing in different directions before you go to bed.

Try all these techniques at once, and the ghosts will probably leave your house and stay away for good.

HOW TO ESCAPE TRICKY SITUATIONS

In a horrible twist of fate, you are mistaken for a spy and seized by undercover agents. You are tied up with rope and placed in the trunk of a car. Here's what you need to do:

THE ROPE ESCAPE

It is important to begin preparing for your escape while you are being tied up. The trick is to make your body take up as much space as possible. Breathe in deeply and push your chest out. Flex and expand your muscles as much as possible. Hopefully this will mean that when you relax and breathe out there will be some slack in the rope. This will make your wriggle to freedom much easier. If your wrists and ankles are being tied, discreetly hold your arms and legs as far apart as you can while they are being bound.

The rope escape is all about getting a feel for the rope. First wriggle a little and try to feel where the ropes are loosening and try to poke out an elbow or an arm. Once one of your arms is free you can begin to work on the knots with your hand.

If your feet are tied, try to slip off your shoes, as this will make getting free much easier.

THE TRUNK ESCAPE

Car trunks are hot and stuffy places, so it is essential to remain calm. Panicking will raise your heart rate and increase your body temperature, which makes the trunk hotter. It will also increase your breathing, which uses up valuable oxygen. Focus your attention on escaping and breathe slowly and regularly.

It sounds obvious, but look for a quick-release mechanism. Many new cars have these installed. It would be located near the catch that keeps the trunk closed, and it may even glow in the dark.

If there is no quick release, look for a trunk release cable. Search under the carpet, or along the sides of the trunk. When you find the cable, pull it to release the catch.

A car's taillights can usually be accessed from inside the trunk. You might have to remove a panel in the trunk to get to them. Once you find the lights, try to push or kick out the unit. This will let in some air and create a space from which you can signal for help to passing cars and pedestrians.

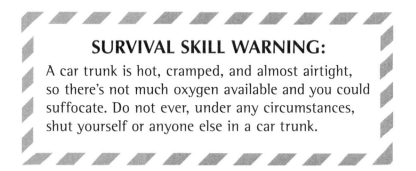

SURVIVAL SKILL WARNING:

A car trunk is hot, cramped, and almost airtight, so there's not much oxygen available and you could suffocate. Do not ever, under any circumstances, shut yourself or anyone else in a car trunk.

HOW TO SURVIVE RADIATION

You have been lucky enough to survive a nuclear explosion. You might be tempted to pat yourself on the back for beating the blast, but you're still facing danger. Radioactive dust produced by the blast will settle on the ground. It will remain radioactive for months or even years after the explosion, and will contaminate everything around the bomb site. Radiation can make you extremely sick and will prove fatal in strong doses. To avoid the radiation, you need to get moving and leave the affected area immediately. Travel as far from it as you can.

Spend as little time outside as possible. As you travel away from the affected area, take shelter in buildings, preferably those made from concrete. Make your bed for the night as far inside a building as possible so that solid materials protect you from the air outside.

Breathing contaminated air is a hazard, but not nearly as dangerous as drinking radiated water or eating contaminated food. Stick to canned food and bottled water until you have put a lot of distance – and that could mean more than 100 miles – between yourself and the location of the explosion.

Wash thoroughly and regularly with soap and water that have not been contaminated. Drink lots of uncontaminated water to help flush radioactive materials from your system.

HOW TO SURVIVE A SWARM OF ANGRY HONEYBEES

On its own, a honeybee is not particularly dangerous unless you are allergic to bee stings. (If you are, and have been stung, seek immediate medical help.) A bee may sting you if it feels threatened (for example if you are about to step on it). Honeybees die after they sting, so they avoid it if possible. But don't be fooled – those black and yellow stripes mean danger. Bee venom packs a punch, and multiple bee stings are very dangerous and can be fatal.

When bees swarm, they can be very aggressive. They want to protect their hive or colony and they are willing to die to do so. Here are some tips about what to do if you encounter a swarm of angry honeybees.

GOOD IDEAS

• Put as much distance as you can between you and the hive. The bees will pursue and sting you until they no longer see you as a threat. Don't stand still – run!

• Take cover in a building if possible, and shut all the doors and windows. If you can't, run through long grass or scrub, which should give you some cover.

BAD IDEAS

• Don't approach a hive. Bees are territorial and more likely to attack if you go near their hive.

• Don't swat at the bees. It will make them sting you more as you are threatening their bee buddies.

• Don't attempt to escape by getting into a body of water. The bees may wait above the water for you to surface.

DEALING WITH STINGS

Gently scrape the stinger out with your fingernail as soon as you can to stop it from injecting more venom. Wash the wound with soap and warm water or rubbing alcohol.

Apply a cold compress to relieve the pain and swelling. A paste of baking soda and water may also soothe the pain.

If you have been unlucky enough to receive more than a dozen stings, or have been stung in or around your mouth or nose, seek medical attention immediately.

HOW TO CATCH A FISH WITH YOUR BARE HANDS

Taking a live fish from water with your bare hands may be illegal where you live, so this is a survival skill that you should only use if you are stranded in the outdoors without any food.

1. Find a stream or river with a good flow of clear water that is no deeper than knee-high.

2. Walk slowly and quietly upstream (which means in the opposite direction to the current) along the bank. Keep low, and look out for fish lying close to the bank, near weeds, and under stones. In running water, stationary fish always face upstream so that water can pass through their gills as they open and close their mouths, allowing them to breathe. Concentrate. Fish are not always easy to spot. Stop and crouch down as soon as you see one – you don't want to scare the fish away. Choose a part of the river or stream where the sun isn't behind you, otherwise your shadow will fall on the water and spook any fish.

3. When you've found a fish close enough to your bank, stay just behind it, out of its sight. Then lie on the bank on your belly. Inch forward toward the edge until you are next to the fish, but don't thump on the bank – fish can feel the vibrations through the water.

4. Next, very slowly and gently so as not to startle the fish, inch your hand and arm into the water until your hand is behind the fish's tail, on the side of the fish away from the bank.

5. Slowly move your hand forward until it is just beneath the fish's gills, and then bring it upward until you are just touching the fish. Move your hand inch by inch, and immediately stop and let the fish settle if it shows signs of being disturbed.

6. Now, using a very light touch, slowly move your hand back along the fish's tummy, and continue to repeat this stroking gesture until the fish starts moving its tail and gills in glee and looking like it is mesmerized.

7. Now act with lightning speed. Quickly and firmly close your hand around the fish just behind the gills, and in the same movement flick it out of the water and onto the bank, far enough away from the edge that it can't wriggle back into the stream.

8. Since you want to eat your catch, take a firm hold of it and kill it at once by knocking it sharply on the top of the head – at a point just behind the eyes – with a stone or heavy stick.

HOW TO GUT A FISH

Preparing a fish you've caught for cooking is very simple. If you do it right, your fish will be safe to eat and free of bad-tasting body parts that might spoil your feast.

GRIME, GUTS, AND GILLS

1. Wash the fish thoroughly in clean, cool running water to get rid of any slime or grit.

2. Gently scrape the blunt side of a sharp knife along the fish from its tail to its head. If the scales spring up, carefully scrape them off, then wash the fish again.

3. Then use the knife to cut off the head behind the gills. Be extremely careful with the knife, as you don't want to end up serving real-life "fish fingers." Turn the fish right-side up and begin by cutting through the backbone behind the head, and then cut through the curve of the gill cover until the head is free.

4. Turn the fish on its back and insert the point of the knife into the vent – the small opening on the underside near the tail. Run the blade up through the skin and thin flesh toward where the head was, opening the fish's body and exposing the insides.

5. Grab a handful of insides at the tail end and pull them out, working toward the head end, until the fish is clear of everything.

6. Carefully use the knife tip to remove the kidney line. This is a dark reddish line that runs along the fish's backbone.

7. Cut off the fins, including, if you want to, the tail. To remove the large fin on the fish's back, insert the knife on one side of the fin, and cut the length of the fin. Do the same on the other side, pulling the fin free at the same time.

8. Wash the fish again, both inside and outside to remove any remaining blood, insides, or other bits.

Wash your hands with soap and hot water after handling raw fish.

Your cleaned fish can now be baked, fried, or barbecued on your campfire. If it's big, you can even cut it into smaller steaks.

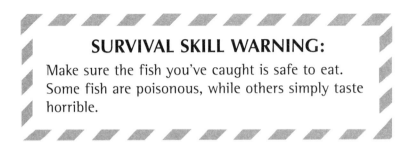

SURVIVAL SKILL WARNING:

Make sure the fish you've caught is safe to eat. Some fish are poisonous, while others simply taste horrible.

HOW TO GET RID OF LEECHES

The bad news is that leeches are bloodsucking, sluglike creatures that lurk in damp places, such as rain forests, tropical jungles, marshes, and swamps, and are just waiting to stick themselves on your skin and gorge themselves on your blood. The good news is that they are not usually harmful, but they can carry bacteria and viruses. So here's how to deal with the little suckers if you need to:

1. In places where leeches are plentiful, if you wade through water they will find you, and if you stand still for a few minutes, you'll see leeches dropping from vegetation and moving toward you. They are attracted

by the sound you make and your scent. Use insect repellent on your skin and clothing. Cover as much of your skin as possible. Full armor is an option, but you will then be in danger of sinking in muddy water!

2. When on an expedition, regularly check your skin to see if any leeches have attached themselves to you.

3. If you find a leech, locate the oral sucker. This is at the thinner end of the leech. Slide a fingernail sideways underneath and scrape the leech off your skin gradually.

4. When the thin end of the leech has been unstuck, quickly slide your finger under the fat end to dislodge it, too. Watch out, as the leech will try hard to reattach itself.

5. Carefully check the rest of your body for more leeches. You never know where they could be hiding.

6. Make sure any wounds on your skin caused by leeches stay clean so they are less likely to become infected.

LEECH DON'TS

• Never wrench a leech off your body. Bits of its jaws might be left behind, imbedded in your skin, and can cause an infection.

• Don't try to burn the leech off or tip salt over it. The leech might let go and fall off, but before it does, it might spit the blood that it has sucked out back into your blood along with all sorts of bacteria.

HOW TO LAND AN AIRPLANE IN AN EMERGENCY

An indulgent godparent has paid for you to have a two-hour flight in a small plane. Forty minutes after taking off, you are cruising at 6,000 feet at a steady 150 mph and enjoying the view of the landscape unfolding beneath you. Suddenly, the pilot suffers a blackout and slumps back in his or her seat, unconscious. Only you can prevent disaster! What should you do?

1. Don't panic! Many small planes have autopilot (a device that, once set and engaged, automatically keeps the plane on a preset course). This will keep the plane flying on the settings the pilot has selected. Even if there is no autopilot, the pilot will have adjusted the plane to fly hands free. This means that the plane will maintain a steady speed, course, and height. Additionally, the pilot will have filed a flight plan, so local air-traffic control (ATC) will be aware of your flight.

2. Make sure the pilot's feet are not obstructing the rudder pedals (these are pretty much where the pedals in a car are). Check that his or her hands or body are not obstructing the control column or yoke (sometimes called the joystick). Most modern light aircraft have dual controls, so you should be able to land the plane from the copilot's seat to the right of the pilot. (If the aircraft has only one set of controls, you will need to drag the pilot out of his or her seat and take over.)

3. Sit down, but don't touch the controls immediately. On the instrument panel in front of you (usually in the center of the top row of instruments in front of the pilot) there is a device called an attitude indicator, also known as an artificial horizon or gyro horizon. This shows the position of the aircraft relative to the ground – that is, whether the wings are level, and whether the aircraft is climbing or descending, or flying at a steady height. It shows a pair of straight lines that represent the plane's wings. Behind them is a sphere or ball divided horizontally; the upper half is usually blue (for the sky) and the lower half is usually brown (for the earth).

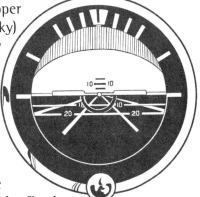

Check to see if the two lines on the attitude indicator representing the aircraft's wings and the white dot between them showing the position of the aircraft's nose line up with the fixed line on the instrument face representing the horizon. If they don't, it means the autopilot is off and the plane is not following a level course.

4. If the autopilot is off, you need to level the plane. Move the yoke in front of you little by little to get the wing lines on the attitude indicator level with the line representing the horizon. Pull the yoke toward you to bring the nose of the plane up. Push it forward to bring the nose down. Move the yoke to the left and the plane will tilt left. Move the yoke to the right and it will tilt right. Do this using gentle movements of the yoke until the plane is flying straight and level. The attitude

indicator will show the wings horizontal and the nose of the aircraft on the line between the SKY and GROUND indicators. Do not use the rudder pedals.

5. There is a radio on the instrument panel, probably in the center. If you can't find a microphone on the instrument panel, take the pilot's headset. Press the PTT (push to talk) button and say "Mayday" three times, clearly and slowly. Then say "Pilot unconscious." Release the PTT button so that the person who receives the call can talk back.

6. Below the radio is the transponder. This identifies the aircraft on radar and will send out your location details so your plane can be tracked by air-traffic control (ATC). Set the dials to 7700 (or type this number in – it is the code for "general emergency"), and ATC will know you have a problem.

7. The controller will give step-by-step instructions on how to land the plane. Follow these carefully, but don't hesitate to ask for things to be repeated if you are at all unsure. Essentially, he or she will instruct you on how to bring the aircraft down to a height from which it can be safely landed. He or she will tell you what to do about controlling engine power, lowering the undercarriage, and turning on to a new course. The controller will talk you through the other instruments, such as the altimeter (which measures the aircraft's height above the ground) and the airspeed indicator. Everything in flying is geared to height, speed, course, and attitude (the angle relative to the earth at which the aircraft is flying), and ATC's instructions will help to keep these four factors correct at any stage during the landing. You might have

to land in a field or on a road, so watch out for power lines and trees, or other obstructions such as bridges.

8. Approach your landing place in a straight line. Just before you reach the ground, pull back slightly on the yoke to lift the nose of the aircraft. This way you'll land on the main wheels beneath the wings. As you slow, the nose wheel will come down.

9. When the plane's main wheels are on the ground, immediately reduce your speed by pulling the throttle (a big black lever between the pilot and copilot seats, or a large knob, usually black, in the lower center of the instrument panel) back toward you. Many light aircraft have toe brakes on the rudder pedals. If your aircraft does, gently press them to bring the plane to a standstill without skidding.

10. There may be a key, like a car's ignition key, on the instrument panel. Once the aircraft has come to a halt, turn this to stop the engine. Do what you can to help the pilot, but wait until the propeller stops turning before attempting to climb out of the aircraft.

HOW TO SURVIVE AN AVALANCHE

An avalanche is an abrupt and rapid flow of snow and debris down a mountain slope. Over a million avalanches happen every year, so they're a serious hazard during any winter expedition in the mountains.

AVOID THE DANGER

Always make sure you carry a snow shovel and an avalanche rescue beacon. The beacon will send out a signal that rescuers can follow if you are buried in snow. Turn the beacon on when you set out on your expedition.

Before crossing a slope, secure your snow goggles, and put on your hat, gloves, and a scarf. Zip up your coat and tighten the neck and cuffs. If an avalanche does happen, it will be harder for the snow to get inside your clothes.

Choose one member of your team to make his or her way across the slope first. Then make sure everyone in your team crosses in the same track. Tell your teammates to concentrate on the snow on the slope above them for any sign of movement.

AVALANCHE!

If you realize an avalanche is about to hit, scream as loud as you can to warn the other members of your team, but when the snow reaches you, close your mouth so you don't swallow any.

Don't try to outrun or outski the avalanche. It may be moving at a speed of more than 80 miles per hour!

Avalanche snow is a bit like water. Once the snow has hit you and knocked you off your feet, try to swim through the snow. You can stay nearer the surface by swimming upward, and this will improve your chances of being rescued. If you can, grab a tree or a rock to stop yourself from sliding down the slope. If you aren't able to grab ahold of anything, curl up in a ball with your hands over your face (to create an air pocket) while the snow covers you.

If you can see light, try to escape, or at least try to reach your hand above the surface where it can be seen. Don't waste valuable energy struggling if you aren't getting anywhere. Your avalanche beacon will be sending out signals giving your location, so remain calm and wait for help.

HOW TO SURVIVE IN BEAR COUNTRY

Bears are as reluctant to bump into you as you are to bump into them. Unfortunately, they often can't resist the smell of the food you have brought on your expedition. It's essential to do everything you can to keep bears from visiting your camp for lunch.

THE BEAR NECESSITIES

1. Never store food or garbage in your tent. Keep it at least 150 feet away from your camp in bear-proof boxes. Alternatively, store your food in an airtight container, put it in a bag, and hang it from the branch of a tree. Select a branch strong enough to support the bag but not a bear climbing on it. Food should be hung at least 10 feet from the ground and at least 4 feet horizontally from the trunk of the tree.

2. Establish your cooking area at least 150 feet away from your camp. Always clean-up thoroughly after eating. Burn or bury all leftover food well away from camp. Dispose of all cooking or clean-up water away from camp, too.

3. Never keep scented items or toiletries in your tent. Toothpaste, soap, deodorant, and lip balm are tasty treats for bears.

4. Don't burn citronella candles (sold to keep insects away). Their lemony scent has been known to attract bears.

5. Never put food out for bears in the hope you will spot one. They will only come closer and closer hoping for more food, and they might get angry when you can't give them any more.

6. When you are out and about, make plenty of noise. Any bears in the area will probably stay out of your way. Clap and sing as you hike. This is particularly important when other noises, such as rushing water, may hide the sound of your footsteps.

BEAR BEWARE!

• If a bear approaches, don't turn and run or shout and scream. Speak in a calm voice and back away with your head tilted downward (but keep your eyes on the bear).

• If a bear attacks you, play dead. Roll onto your stomach and clasp your hands behind your neck. Stay in this position until the bear leaves the area. If it doesn't show signs of leaving you alone, or becomes more ferocious, fight it off with all your might.

HOW TO BUILD A SURVIVAL SHELTER

This easy survival shelter can be made in a couple of hours, provided you have a tarp. It will keep you warm and dry, and will help you get a good night's sleep, which is vital to preserving your strength and maintaining a positive attitude if you are stranded in the wilderness. Here's how to build it:

1. Find two strong, straight sticks, each with a fork at one end. Make sure they are the same length (about 4 feet). Sharpen the unforked ends and dig them firmly into the ground to a depth of at least 15 inches and 6 feet apart. If one stick is longer than the other, dig it farther into the ground to even up the height.

2. Find another long, straight stick that is at least 6 feet long and rest this in the forks of the upright sticks. This is your ridge pole. Secure it to the forked sticks with twine.

3. Throw the tarp over the ridge pole to make a tent. If it is large enough, use some of the tarp to form a floor for you to make your bed on.

4. Peg the tarp down with sticks, or place heavy stones along the wall edges to keep it secure.

AN ALTERNATIVE SHELTER

If you don't have a tarp, make a shelter by building two walls out of branches and poles.

1. Find a long pole or branch (about one and a half

times your height). Find a tree with a forked branch to support your shelter at one end.

2. Place the pole against the tree, then place smaller poles on each side of the main pole to make a sloping framework. Next, weave some thin, bendy branches through the small poles to make a criss-cross frame.

3. Cover your frame with materials such as dead leaves, dry ferns, moss, and grass. Add some light branches to the outside of the shelter to keep your insulating material from blowing away. Then spread a thick layer of dry grass on the floor of the shelter for you to sleep on.

HOW TO SURVIVE A VISIT FROM AN ABOMINABLE SNOWMAN

Picture yourself trekking through the Himalayas in Tibet. There are many dangers you will have prepared for before setting out – the cold, snowy conditions, the treacherous, rocky landscape, and the low oxygen levels that you will find at this high altitude. What you might have forgotten to prepare for, however, is a visit from an abominable snowman (also known as a yeti).

Some people don't actually believe that yetis exist, but just in case you encounter one, here are some rules to follow:

1. Never enter into a long discussion with a yeti about whether or not you believe in yetis. This is guaranteed to make a yeti very angry. Imagine if you had trekked across a wild and desolate landscape in search of food or company only to be told that you don't exist. Wouldn't that make you abominably bad-tempered?

2. Don't run around screaming or throwing things at the yeti. Yetis are bigger and stronger than you, and if you make them angry, they may attack. Stay calm and slowly back away with your arms out in front of you, your hands clearly visible and your palms down. This will put the yeti at ease and show it that you are not about to reach for something to throw at it.

3. Some people believe yetis are the distant cousins of human beings. So why not offer the yeti a cup of hot cocoa or some food? Snow people are often amazed by

our abominable lack of manners when receiving guests. When a yeti has guests, it will always offer some wild rhododendron tea and a few snow cookies even if the guest shows up uninvited.

4. Don't flash cameras in a yeti's face – snow people find this very rude. Always ask the yeti's permission before taking its photograph so it has enough time to arrange its fur in a pleasing way. If you ask the yeti nicely enough, it may even let you pose in the shot as well.

HOW TO TIE A QUICK-RELEASE KNOT

This quick-release knot is ideal for tying up something for a brief period of time, such as a hammock that you want to have a quick nap in. The knot will stay put, but if you tug on the loose end you can make it unravel easily.

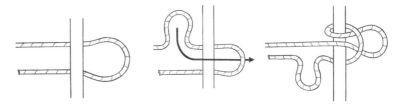

1. Put a loop around a post or tree.

2. Make a kink and pass it through your loop.

3. Make another kink from the lower end of the rope.

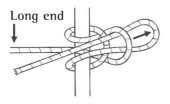

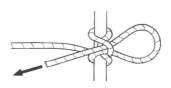

4. Pass this kink through the first kink. Pull on the long end of the rope to secure the knot.

5. To release the knot, pull on the short end.

HOW TO SEND AN SOS

If you find yourself in need of rescuing, whether stranded on land or at sea, your priority is to attract the attention of potential rescuers. You need to send out an urgent signal for help called an SOS. Here are some ways to do this:

FIRE, FIRE!

Fires are effective if they are built in a clearing. By day, the smoke can be seen for miles. By night, the light from a fire will be visible from even farther away. Three fires arranged in the shape of a triangle is a well-known distress signal. Add leaves, fresh grass, ferns, and damp wood to your fires to produce smoke, which will increase visibility during daylight. Use drier wood for a brighter blaze at night.

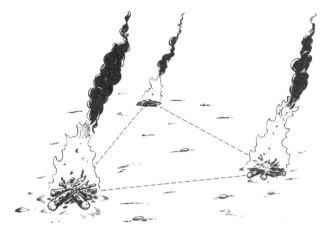

Make sure there is nothing nearby that can catch fire if your signal fires flare up or blow out sparks, and don't build any fires in a dry or wooded area. Never signal for help unless you genuinely need it or you might spark a false rescue attempt. When you have finished signaling, remember to put out your signal fires by covering them with soil or pouring water on them until all the embers have stopped glowing.

GOT THE MESSAGE?

Morse code uses a combination of long and short pulses of light or sound to communicate letters and numbers. An SOS in Morse code can be sent using a flashlight. Alternatively, you can use a shiny surface, such as a mirror or a polished piece of metal, to reflect sunlight. Direct your flashes of light toward the ship or aircraft you are trying to attract.

To send an SOS in Morse code, repeat this sequence: three short flashes, three longer flashes, three short flashes.

PLANE SPOTTER

To make sure you alert a passing helicopter or plane to your location, make a large signal on the ground that can be seen from the air. Reflective materials, such as metal

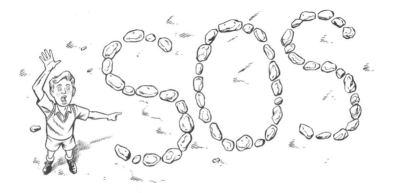

wreckage from a car or plane, or any brightly colored materials, are ideal. Use branches or stones if that's all you can find. Arrange the objects so they spell out SOS, or form a geometric shape, such as a triangle or square. In nature, objects rarely form regular shapes, so a search party is much more likely to notice an unnatural, human-made arrangement of objects.

Stop signaling if you are certain that your signal has been seen otherwise you might confuse your original SOS or dazzle the pilot of an aircraft.

When you are rescued, make sure any SOS signals that you have made on the ground are cleared away. That way nobody else will see them and think someone needs help.

HOW TO SURVIVE A ZOMBIE INVASION

Should it happen, a zombie attack is probably the hardest challenge you will ever face. Zombies (or the "undead," as they prefer to be known) are notoriously difficult to kill because they are not actually alive. As soon as you hear reports of zombies in your area, follow this plan of action.

GAME PLAN

Gather as many survivors of the invasion as you can; there is safety in numbers. Find a secure building to use as a base. Ideally, it should be on high ground. This will offer an excellent vantage point from which you can spot zombie hordes approaching, and the undead can't climb because their knees don't bend. Stock plenty of food and water, as you may be surrounded by the undead for days.

Make sure the building has only two entrances (you need a second door to use to escape if zombies break through the front entrance). Build a barricade at each entrance and seal any other doors and windows with heavy furniture.

HOW TO SPOT A ZOMBIE

The living dead are easy to spot because, as their name suggests, they are dead people whose bodies have come alive again. Look out for staring eyes, green skin, and a pungent smell of rotting and decay. Check for a distinctive way of walking – slowly stumbling with arms held straight out in front and a limp caused by their stiff knees.

If survivors come to your base asking for shelter, beware. They may have been infected. This happens if they are bitten or scratched by a zombie. There is no cure. They will become zombies, too. Check all newcomers for any wounds.

If someone has been infected, you must get him or her out of your safe house quickly. The good news is once he or she is a full-blown zombie he or she won't feel pain and he or she will never be forced to do anything he or she doesn't want to again. The bad news is he or she will stink and his or her flesh will fall off.

BATTLING WITH THE UNDEAD

After a while you may get bored of waiting it out in a barricaded base. Television broadcasts will eventually stop, and there'll be nothing but the sound of static on the radio. You may decide to venture outside. Be very careful. Whenever you leave the shelter to gather fresh supplies or check for more survivors, carry a bat or sword to defend yourself. Guns are useless against zombies. You can knock a zombie's head off and stop it in its tracks, though.

If you find yourself caught in a crowd of the undead, your best chance of surviving is to act like a zombie. Moan and keep your eyes as wide open as possible. Limp and drool. Zombies are pretty stupid, and with any luck they won't notice you among them.

HOW TO ESCAPE FROM QUICKSAND

Quicksand is a thick sludge that is most commonly found near beaches or rivers. In the movies, people slowly sink into it, unable to escape, until their heads finally disappear beneath the surface and they're never seen again.

In reality, getting stuck in quicksand doesn't mean an inevitable death. It is often only a couple of feet deep and you'll stop sinking when your feet touch the solid bottom.

BE PREPARED

Most people who perish in quicksand die by drowning. This is because quicksand is usually found in tidal areas. When the tide comes in, the area is submerged underwater, as is anyone stuck in the sand. The most important thing is to be prepared and not allow yourself to get stuck.

• If you know or suspect there is quicksand in an area, take an alternate route.

• If you are traveling in a group, spread out. Make sure you walk with a ten-step gap between each team member. This way if one of you starts sinking the others can stop and help rather than sink in with you.

• Use a stick to prod and test the ground in front of you.

• Carry a length of rope that you can use to lasso nearby objects in order to pull yourself out in an emergency.

ESCAPING A STICKY SITUATION

As soon as you feel you are sinking, throw away any heavy objects you are carrying, such as your backpack. You must avoid allowing your feet to plunge down into the sand under the weight of your body. Quickly lean your whole body backward until you are lying flat. This will spread out your weight and help you float on the surface of the sand. Breathe in deeply and fill your lungs with air to increase your buoyancy.

Lie still. Don't thrash around. Any sudden movements will stir up the quicksand and make it less stable. Wait for the sand to settle around you. Carefully maneuver your walking stick underneath your hips, so you are lying across it. It will help keep you on the surface.

Stay on your back, but use your arms and legs to swim, crawl, and drag yourself toward solid ground. Move very slowly, inching your way to firmer ground.

HOW TO TRACK A WILD ANIMAL

Before you can track down a wild animal, you must be able to recognize its footprints. Memorize the animal tracks below, then read on for how to find each animal.

Here are some tracks you won't mind finding:

dog   cat   fox   badger   running rabbit

Here are some tracks you should not follow:

hyena   bear   hippo   mountain lion

TRACKER TIPS

• The best time to go tracking is early in the morning or late in the day. When the sun is low in the sky, tracks will be edged with shadow, making them more visible.

• Always take a tracking guidebook with you so you can identify any unusual tracks you come across.

• Scout around for tracks. Brush loose leaves and vegetation aside. Keep an eye out for animal trails. These are routes that animals take regularly where soil and vegetation will appear to be worn down.

• When you find a trail of prints, mark each one by pushing a stick into the ground next to it. This will help you to see the animal's stride pattern. From this, you will be able to speculate on the size and type of animal you are tracking.

• Use a magnifying glass to look closely at the prints. You might find an animal has a clipped hoof or damaged claw that makes its track unique. This will help you distinguish your animal's track from that of other, similar animals.

• Look out for droppings, chewed plants, and any other signs of the animal's activity. This will help you identify the animal you are following. The droppings, for example, might have a distinctive smell.

• Don't look down at your feet. You'll track down the animal much faster if you look between 10 and 20 feet away from your body.

• Stay low, move slowly, and be as quiet as you can. Even the sound of a snapping twig could make the animal you are tracking run off.

ON THE RIGHT TRACK

As you get closer to the animal you are tracking, its footprints will become cleaner, with less spare dirt, twigs,

and leaves lying on top of them. Its droppings, being fresher, will be warmer and softer. At this point, slow down in case you come across the animal and startle it.

If you need to hide, take refuge in a bush and get down on your hands and knees. If you are unable to do that, lie down in some long grass and inch along the ground using your arms.

If the wind is behind you, you might want to leave the trail and creep around to the side of the animal's tracks so that your scent doesn't get blown toward the animal and scare it away.

HOW TO MAKE A TRACKING STICK

Animal tracking is great fun, and this tracking stick will help you master the art.

1. Find a branch that is about 3 feet long.

2. Use this to measure the distance between one footprint and the next footprint left by the same foot, from heel to heel. This will give you the length of the animal's stride. Use a sharp stone to scratch a mark on your stick in the position of each heel (X and Z).

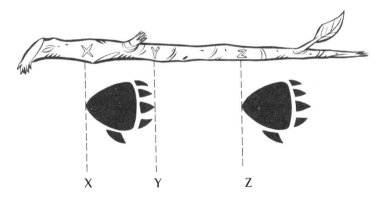

3. Hold the stick with point X at the heel of the first footprint and measure the length of this print. Use your stone to mark the front of the print as point Y.

4. To begin using the stick, hold it so that point X is over the heel of the rearmost print and then look close to point Z for the next track. Repeat this process until you track down your animal.

HOW TO STAGE A JAILBREAK

You are in a faraway country and find yourself imprisoned (obviously due to an unfortunate misunderstanding and through absolutely no mistake of your own) in a lonely prison cell. Don't despair. Instead, start planning your escape.

THE BREAKOUT

Brick walls are among the easiest walls to escape through:

1. Scrape out the mortar around a single brick using a key, a spoon, or any sharp object. This will take days. When you're not working on the brick, mix the scraped-out mortar with water or spit and push it back into place. This will make the brick look untouched.

Choose a brick that is hidden from view by your bed or a piece of furniture, and make sure you cover it up after every scraping session.

2. Once one brick is out, the bricks around it will be a lot easier to remove. Only take out the minimum number of bricks you need to form a hole through which you can squeeze.

3. When it comes to the actual escape, you'll need to figure out your guards' routine. They will check your cell at regular intervals. You'll need to time your escape immediately after they have visited, thus giving you the maximum time to get away before they check your cell again. The best time to escape is at night, because the number of guards patrolling outside your cell will be at a minimum and your movements will be under the cover of darkness. When you are ready to go, make it look like you are still in your bed by putting pillows or spare clothes under your blanket. If you're lucky, the guards might not know you've escaped until morning. By then, you'll be long gone.

4. As you leave your cell, reach back through the hole and pull the furniture back in front of it, so that it can't be easily seen from your cell door.

SURVIVAL SKILL WARNING:

Don't ever try to escape through your bedroom wall. Your room will get drafty and someone is bound to spot the hole sooner or later, and it will probably be your parents, who won't be amused!

HOW TO MAKE A GETAWAY

You are on the run and need to put as much distance between yourself and your pursuers as possible. Here's how:

DISGUISE YOUR TRACKS

Try not to leave an obvious trail. Stick to roads, rocks, and other hard surfaces where you won't leave noticeable footprints. If you can't avoid leaving prints, don't waste a lot of time brushing them away. It is essential to move quickly, and brush marks are easy to spot.

Backtracking (walking backward in your own tracks) is an excellent way to confuse trackers:

1. Find a starting spot that will make your trail harder to follow – such as a slab of stone or some shallow water.

2. Walk up to this spot, then walk backward in your own tracks for ten steps.

3. Leap sideways off your trail and set off in a completely different direction. If the start of your new trail is hidden by a tree or bush, that's even better.

ON THE SCENT

If your pursuers are using tracker dogs, your chances of a clean getaway are smaller unless you can throw the dogs off your scent.

• Scramble over fences or walls that will be hard for the dogs to scale.

• Whenever possible, stay downwind of the dogs so they can't pick up your scent.

• Wade through water at every opportunity. This is the most effective way to leave no tracks and no scent.

• If you come to a stream, don't go straight across; if you have time, walk or swim up or downstream for a good distance before getting out on the other bank.

• Whenever possible, mingle with other people in a crowded place, so that your scent will be mixed with the scents of others.

• Best of all, if you can get yourself on a horse or a bicycle you will break your trail, and it will be very difficult for a dog to sniff you out.

HOW TO SURVIVE A SCHOOL DANCE

Picture the scene: Terrible music is playing, lights are flashing, your teachers are desperately trying to look cool, and there are girls everywhere. Girls who want to dance with you.

If this situation doesn't bother you, select the girl you want to dance with. Ask her confidently but nicely to dance. Whisk her onto the dance floor. Whirl her around in time to the music, and show off your coolest dance moves.

THINGS TO SAY TO IMPRESS YOUR PARTNER

- *"Do you do modeling for extra cash?"* • *"Do you dance professionally?"* • *"That color really suits you."*

THINGS NOT TO SAY

- *"What's that in your hair?"* • *"Where's that smell coming from?"* • *"My friends dared me to ask you to dance."*

EVASIVE ACTION

If the very thought of girls or dancing sends shivers down your spine, you have two options. You can stay at home, watch TV, feed your goldfish, and go to bed early. Or you can go to the dance, but bandage one leg or one arm heavily. Stand at the side of the room and look as though you would love to dance, but you simply can't.

Survival Tip: If you'd rather dance by yourself, you'll need a strategy to keep the girls at a distance. Fling your arms around wildly, get really into the music, and sing along loudly. You'll find a wide circle opening up around you.

HOW TO MAKE A SLINGSHOT

Slingshots are great for firing small stones at tin cans in your backyard or for scaring off ferocious animals that may attack your camp in the wilderness. Your handy little sling could even come in useful for fending off invading aliens or zombies.

SLINGSHOT CONSTRUCTION

1. Find a strong but flexible forked branch (about an inch thick). An evenly Y-shaped branch works best.

2. Next you will need a large rubberband. Alternatively, use a bit of the inner tube of a bike's tire. This will be stronger than a rubberband.

3. Find a strong, oblong piece of fabric, big enough to hold a large marshmallow. Leather or denim will work well. Thread your elastic through two holes in the fabric so that the pouch sits in the middle as shown below.

4. Tie an end of the elastic sling to each prong of your forked stick.

5. Hold your finished slingshot at the base and place a small stone or a marshmallow in the fabric pouch.

6. Pull back on the sling until the elastic is fully stretched. Aim through the V made by the two upper arms of the slingshot. Then let go of the sling to fire the slingshot.

You'll need to practice if you want to hit a tin can.

SURVIVAL SKILL WARNING:

Never fire your slingshot at another person or animal. Always wear protective eyewear and be sure an adult is present when you use your slingshot. Slingshots may be illegal where you live, so be sure to check your local laws before you make one.

HOW TO SURVIVE A HUGE PIMPLE

Have you ever woken up to find a pimple the size of a volcano taking over your face? You don't have to barricade yourself in your room for days. Instead, deal with it.

• Be realistic. Your zit really won't look as big to anyone else as it does to you. Your friends might not even notice it.

• To prevent the pimple from getting infected and swollen, don't rub, squeeze, or pick at it. This will just make it worse.

• Dab your zit with medicated cream or some diluted tea tree oil.

• There are lots of other ways to get rid of pimples. There are weird remedies, such as washing your face in rose water during a full moon while standing on your head. Feel free to try this if you want to. Rose water might not make any difference to your pimples, but girls will think you smell lovely.

• To prevent more pimples, make sure you drink plenty of water and eat at least five portions of fresh fruit and vegetables a day.

• Keep your skin clean by washing your face with a gently medicated face wash every day and pat it dry with a clean, soft towel.

HOW TO CARRY SOMEONE TO SAFETY

If someone in your expedition team has sprained his or her ankle but is still conscious and can hold himself or herself upright, you can make a stable seat with your hands simply by joining forces with another person.

1. Following the picture shown above, place your right hand on your left wrist, and grip tightly. Ask your lifting partner to do the same.

2. Now grip your partner's right wrist with your left hand and get him or her to grip your right wrist. (Follow the picture shown on the opposite page.)

3. Lower your joined hands by bending your legs, not your backs.

4. Get your injured friend to sit on the four-handed seat and place his or her arms tightly around both of the lifters' shoulders.

5. When the injured person is seated, stand up, making sure you keep your backs straight.

6. As soon as you have carried the injured person to safety, find a trained medical professional who can examine him or her.

SAFETY POINTS

• Do not lift anyone who may have a serious injury unless it is absolutely necessary. For example, if the person is facing oncoming danger, such as a fire, it's probably a good idea to lift him or her.

• Always ask someone else for help when lifting. Don't try to lift an injured person on your own or you could end up dropping him or her and doing more damage.

HOW TO MAKE AN UNDERWATER ESCAPE

You are deep in the mountains on a road trip when suddenly the biggest, grizzliest bear lumbers in front of your car. You swerve to avoid it, and your car veers off the road, plunging into a nearby lake.

You're in trouble, but you're not doomed. You will have to move quickly, though, as a car can sink in just 60 seconds. Immediately remove your seat belt so you are ready for action. Help any small children in the car remove their seatbelts.

As soon as your car hits the water, lower your windows as quickly as possible. Electric windows should still work while your car is afloat, and they may continue to work if you are submerged in fresh water. Climb out of a window and swim to safety as quickly as possible.

If you are unable to open your windows, try to smash one open. If you have a spring-loaded center punch, use it. Otherwise, use something heavy, such as a wrench or the metal end of a headrest. Smash it at the corner, as this is where the window is weakest.

If the car sinks before you can do any of the above, you are going to have to wait until the car has filled with water. This will equalize the pressure of the water inside and outside the car. Climb into the backseat because the front of the car, where the heavy engine is, will sink first. Wait until the water has reached neck height. Then instruct everyone to take a big gulp of air. Once the doors

are completely submerged, they should open with a push.
Try shoving a door with your feet while steadying yourself
by grabbing onto a seat. Exit the car, and swim away and
up to the surface.

HOW TO SURVIVE THE BUBONIC PLAGUE

In the unlikely event that you wake up in medieval or Elizabethan England and discover that an epidemic of the bubonic plague has reached your town or village, here are some tips on how to survive it.

SURVIVAL STRATEGIES

• Symptoms of the plague include a headache, aching joints, a fever, and vomiting. Large lumps will appear around your armpits, neck, and groin area, and black spots will appear on your skin. These are the "buboes" from which the plague takes its name. Watch out for these symptoms in yourself and your family.

• Keep your house clean. By dropping food crumbs on the floor of your kitchen, you may attract rats with fleas that are carrying the bubonic plague.

• Don't copy your ancestors and carry flowers around with you because you think they will prevent you from getting the plague. They might cover up the smell of rotting plague victims, but they certainly won't keep you from catching the dreaded disease.

COPING WITH AN OUTBREAK

• Shut yourself in your house, but get word to anyone who has been near you that you have the plague so they can get some medical help.

• Do not stop bathing. It is essential that you keep your sores really clean so they are less likely to become infected.

• Paint a red cross on your door. This will tell your friends that your household has become infected with the plague and they will know not to visit you after school.

• Alternatively, you could try to survive until the twentieth century when antibiotics will be available and your chances of survival will be much greater.

HOW TO SURVIVE A SHOPPING EXPEDITION

It is a bright sunny holiday weekend and you are looking forward to going to the park with your friends. You go into the kitchen for your breakfast when Mom drops a bombshell: *"I think we should go out to get you some new clothes for school today."*

AARRGGH! This is not what you planned for your day, but don't despair. Follow these tips and you could be at the park before lunchtime.

Shopping is like any other expedition, and careful planning will help you avoid disaster. Establish a clear objective. What are you shopping for and where are you going for it? This is essential to avoid wandering around stores that don't even sell the things you need.

Establish how long you are going to be out. If your parent is vague on this, beware. He or she could be planning a whole-day trip. Think of reasons the trip should be brief:

- *"You said you were going to call so and so . . ."*
- *"Your friend from aerobics said she might stop by after lunch."*
- *"That movie you wanted to watch is on this afternoon."*

Get yourself ready quickly, and then get any younger brothers or sisters who are coming with you ready. It's true that the sooner you head out, the sooner you will be back. If you set out early in the morning, you will miss the traffic and the stores will be empty, with no long lines.

Decide how important a day at the park is to you. Think about this very carefully. Are you prepared to wear flared pants that are three sizes too big and a giant itchy sweater that you "will grow into" to school every day for the next two years? If so, agree to everything your mom wants to buy and you will be done in no time. Your mom may even drop you off at the park on your way home.

HOW TO AVOID A HUNGRY HIPPO

You're on an African safari when, out of nowhere, a hungry, 2-ton hippo appears. Hippos can spend up to sixteen hours a day chilling out in water, but don't be fooled. They are extremely aggressive, fiercely territorial, and very fast. A hippo can run at speeds of up to 18 miles an hour.

In short, there's not a great deal you can do to defend yourself against a hippo attack, so your best policy is to avoid one. Here's how:

• If you encounter a hippo on dry land, don't startle it. Walk away as quietly and quickly as possible.

• Never get between a mother hippo and her baby. Female hippos are extremely protective of their young.

• Don't sail down an African river where hippos can be found. Hippos attack people who disturb them when they are having a soak. They can hold their breath underwater for five minutes, so just because you can't see a hippo, it doesn't mean that the coast is clear.

• Never jump in the water to swim with a hippo. Bathing like a hippo might look like fun, but you aren't a hippo and there's no way you'll fool the hippo into thinking that you are, no matter how good you are at holding your breath.

HOW TO TIE A SLING

1. Find a large piece of clean fabric, about 3 square feet. A pillowcase cut open into a square is ideal. Fold the fabric in half diagonally to make a triangle-shaped sling.

2. Hold the fabric under the injured person's arm, placing one end over the opposite shoulder.

3. Bring the other end of the fabric up over the arm, and over the other shoulder.

4. Tie the two ends together at the back of the injured person's neck, making sure the arm is held gently but securely in place.

5. Use a safety pin to fasten the remaining corner of the fabric. Pin the corner to the sling near the elbow.

Survival Tip: If you can't find a piece of fabric to use to make your sling, try using a piece of clothing such as a sweater.

You might need to practice tying your sling a few times before you get it right, so find a willing friend to practice on.

HOW TO SURVIVE AN ESSAY CRISIS

Help! Your essay is due in the morning and you've been playing video games all evening. Here's how to save your skin by whipping up an excellent essay in no time.

1. Think carefully about what you want to say. Scribble down some ideas. Then join up any ideas that are linked.

2. Organize your ideas on a big piece of paper. If you are presenting some information, divide it into categories. For example, if your subject is the history of exploration, you could have "The First Explorers," "Exploration Today," and "What Is There Left to Discover?" Jot them down as headings, leaving plenty of space beneath each one.

3. List the main points that should go under each heading. Next to each point, list any facts that back it up.

4. Write an introduction. It might seem odd that writing an introduction is the fourth step, but now is a good time because you know what is in the essay. Just give a brief summary of your essay. Don't explain what you have found out, though – you should include that in the conclusion.

5. Write your conclusion last. If you have presented an argument (such as "Why I should lead a team to the North Pole"), round it off by summarizing the main points of the argument that you have already mentioned. For example: "I would be the youngest explorer to make the journey. As a result, people would give me lots of money to finance the trip. I would look really cool in the newspapers pictured standing at the North Pole."

6. Hand in your essay with a proud grin and wait for your teacher to give you a great grade.

HOW TO SURVIVE BEING STUCK IN AN ELEVATOR

If you find yourself stuck in an elevator, remain calm. You are not in a movie, and a modern elevator is very unlikely to come crashing down, even if the cables snap. Modern elevators also don't have hatches in the ceiling through which you can escape. This is a good thing because escaping through a hatch would be very dangerous.

Press each of the floor buttons one by one. Then try the DOOR OPEN button. If none of these buttons work, the elevator is broken and you need to let someone know about it.

Look for an emergency telephone. If there isn't one, look for an ALARM button. Press this repeatedly. Someone should hear you and get help. You can also use a cell phone to call 911 and ask for help.

If you can see light through any gap between the elevator doors, the elevator has probably stopped near a floor and you can try to shout for help. The doors can be opened with a key. Don't ever try to force them open yourself.

If you don't have a cell phone and you have waited for more than half an hour and nobody has arrived to help, shout and bang on the walls of the elevator with a set of keys or a shoe. If there are still people in the building, you need to get their help before they leave for the night.

If everyone has left the building and nobody is responding to the alarm, the worst-case scenario is that you could be in the elevator overnight. If this happens, don't panic. Make yourself comfortable and get some sleep (and hope you don't need to use the bathroom!)

HOW TO SURVIVE A SNAKEBITE

Not all snakes are poisonous, and even poisonous snakes don't always inject venom into a victim when they bite. However, always assume a snake is poisonous, just in case.

In the movies, the hero usually cuts his buddy's snakebite with a knife and sucks out the poison. Don't do this. You might make yourself sick, and cutting the flesh around the bite might help the venom to spread and could cause infection.

Get to a hospital as fast as you can. Even if you don't immediately feel unwell, it is essential that you get medical treatment as quickly as possible. If the bite starts to swell up and changes color, it means the snake that bit you was probably poisonous.

Make a note of the exact time of the bite and of the size and appearance of the snake. This information will help the doctors who treat the bite. If possible, telephone the hospital with these details before you get there so they can have the correct treatment ready when you arrive.

SELF-TREATMENT

If you can't get medical attention immediately, remain calm. Panicking will increase your heart rate, and this will help the venom spread through your body faster.

Take the following precautions:

• If you've been bitten on your arm or hand, remove your watch. Your hand or wrist might swell up and your watch could become painfully stuck. Remove any other pieces of tight clothing that are near the bite.

• Dress the wound with a bandage that fits snugly, but not too tightly. You want to slightly restrict the flow of blood to the bitten area, but not cut off the blood supply altogether.

• If you're with another member of your expedition party, get them to wash your bite with soap and water. Lie down flat so that the area of your body that was bitten is not higher than your heart. This will slow down the speed at which venom travels to this vital part of your body. Tell them to tie a splint to the affected limb. This will restrict its movement and help prevent the venom from moving around the body.

HOW TO AVOID A MAN-EATING TIGER

Tigers usually don't attack and eat humans unless they are old or injured and unable to hunt for other food. However, in some rare cases, a single tiger that has turned into a "man-eater" has been known to kill dozens or even hundreds of people.

TIGER TIPS

You find out that a man-eating tiger is on the loose in your vicinity, and may find its way to your camp, town, or village. Here's how to prepare for and deal with the danger:

1. Make a papier-mâché face mask. Wear it on the back of your head, not your face, so you look as if you have two faces — one at the front and one at the back. A tiger doesn't like to jump on its prey from the front and your mask will confuse it.

2. Carry a club over your right shoulder at all times. Tigers attack humans on the back of their necks, so you will be ready to defend yourself.

3. If you catch sight of the tiger just before it pounces, turn to face it and look it right in the eye.

4. If you see the tiger in the distance, make a run for it. Tigers won't try to chase you over long distances. If a tiger thinks you have already seen it and you are quite far away, it might just leave you alone and wait for another piece of meat to come along.

Survival Tip: Don't bother leaping into the village pond or local pool, and don't climb a tree or scramble on top of a bus shelter to escape a tiger. Tigers are excellent swimmers and climbers, so it will soon catch up with you.

HOW TO PREDICT RAIN

Knowing whether or not it is going to rain is an invaluable skill when leading an expedition. Rain can make surfaces dangerous and your team's progress slow, plus your friends will appreciate staying dry!

Sometimes all you need to do is take a quick look at your teammates' hair to judge whether the weather is about to change. Some people with curly hair will find their hair curls up more tightly before it rains.

Alternatively, most flowers are quick to open up when rain threatens. Regularly check the air to tell if the scent of any nearby blooms has become noticeably stronger.

Stay alert to unusual animal behavior, too. Animals are often aware of differences in air pressure, which indicate a change in the weather. If you notice that buzzing insects have suddenly gone quiet or that birds have returned to the trees, it's probably a sign that you're about to get drenched and it's time for you to seek shelter as well.

CLOUD READING

Gray clouds in the sky don't necessarily mean that a heavy shower is brewing, but the skies can give you essential information about the weather. Check the following:

Time of day. A gray morning sky can actually be a sign of a glorious day to come, but if the sky turns gray and clouds over later in the afternoon, it means rain is probable.

Shape. Thin and wispy clouds that are spaced far apart signal fine weather. When they gather together and get ominously larger, they are likely to produce rain quite suddenly.

Height. As a general rule, the higher a cloud is in the sky, the better the weather will be. A covering of low, dark clouds is usually bad news, suggesting a lengthy downpour is probably on the way.

Color. Clouds that are dark underneath and very tall usually mean that thunder, lightning, hail, and strong winds are plotting to wreak havoc.

HOW TO BUILD AN IGLOO

1. Use a stick to mark a circle in the snow that is about 11 feet across. Grab a snow shovel and dig out the circle to a depth of about 6 inches. Trample down the circle of snow with your feet.

2. Find a large, clear area of deep snow nearby and jump on it until it is flat. This is going to be your snow quarry.

3. Use your shovel to cut out some snow bricks about 28 inches long, 20 inches wide, and 8 inches deep.

4. Build a layer of snow bricks around the outside of your circle. Shape the bricks so that the row makes a spiral shape. Be sure to leave a gap for the entrance. Get a friend to work from the inside of the igloo, filling in the cracks with snow.

5. Build a second layer of bricks, cutting each brick so that they continue to make a spiral. Then create more layers of bricks until you have an igloo shape with a hole at the top.

6. Cap the hole with a single block of packed snow. Cut a block that is slightly bigger than the hole and get your partner to help lift it up and put it in place.

7. Climb inside the igloo and trim the cap so that it fits the hole. Pack snow around the edges of the cap.

8. Dig a little trench in the snow leading up to the entrance hole.

9. Make an arch over your entrance hole by placing two narrow bricks on either side. Make sure the arch will be big enough for you to crawl through easily.

10. Make a few airholes in the roof of the igloo. These are essential for avoiding suffocation.

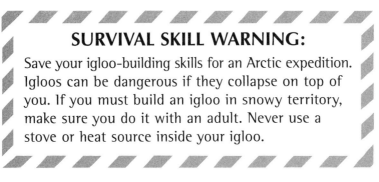

SURVIVAL SKILL WARNING:

Save your igloo-building skills for an Arctic expedition. Igloos can be dangerous if they collapse on top of you. If you must build an igloo in snowy territory, make sure you do it with an adult. Never use a stove or heat source inside your igloo.

HOW TO MAKE FRESH WATER FROM SEAWATER

If you are marooned on a desert island after a shipwreck, you'll be surrounded by water. Annoyingly, you won't be able to drink any of it because it will be full of salt. With any luck, you will have salvaged some useful utensils from the wreck of the ship, such as cooking pots and tin cans. Now you can make fresh, delicious drinking water from salty seawater.

1. Stand a clean, empty tin can on the bottom of an empty cooking pot or bowl. Place a stone in the can to keep it in place.

2. Pour seawater into the pot until the level is about three quarters the height of the can. Make sure the seawater does not enter the can.

3. Put the pot's lid on upside down, so that the lid handle is over the empty can inside. Put the pot over a campfire and wait for the water to boil.

4. As the water boils, carefully pour a little cold seawater over the lid of the pot to keep it cool. Make sure that your fire doesn't go out. As the water boils, it turns to steam and leaves the salt particles behind in the pan. The steam collects on the inside of the lid and, as it cools, condenses into pure water droplets. The condensation then runs down the lid's handle, dripping into the can. Keeping the outside of the lid cool with cold water makes the steam condense faster.

5. After twenty minutes, use some twigs as tongs to lift the lid of the pot and check the water's progress. Once the can is almost full, very carefully remove it from the pot with the tongs. The pot, can, and water will be very hot.

6. Let the can of water cool before drinking.

SURVIVAL SKILL WARNING:

Don't try doing this unless you have been shipwrecked. Seawater tastes disgusting and is extremely bad for you if it has not been boiled in the correct way because it contains huge amounts of salt.

HOW TO LIGHT A FIRE

There are several ways to make a fire if you don't have any matches or a lighter. The "fire-bow drill" is a clever version of the "rubbing two sticks together" method. Here's how to do it:

1. Collect some tinder. Tinder is anything that catches fire very easily, such as dry, thin grass, cotton fluff, and dry pine needles. You will need a good handful to start your fire.

2. Find a wooden stick for your bow. It needs to be a strong stick that is about 2 feet long and about 1/2 inch wide. It must be quite stiff but still bendable. A thin bamboo cane is good for this.

3. Now you will need some cord or string. A shoelace is perfect if it is long enough. Carefully carve a slight notch around each end of the bow. Attach the cord to the bow at either end around the notches. The cord should be stretched tightly enough to make the bow bend slightly (see picture on the next page).

4. The drill should be a piece of hard, dry branch about 12 inches long and 1 inch wide. It should have a sharp point at one end and be rounded and blunt at the other. The straighter your drill, the easier it will be to use. Twist the drill into your cord (see picture on the next page).

5. Make a base called a fireboard. You will need a flat piece of soft, dry wood that is 1 inch thick, 6 inches wide, and 2 feet long.

6. Carve a V-shaped notch in one end of the board about 1 inch deep and 1 inch wide, as shown below. Put your tinder in the notch.

7. Make a hole in the board that is about the same width as your drill and 1/2 inch deep. The hole should be centered near the notch you made.

8. Find a stone with a natural hollow in it that is about the same size as the blunt end of your fire drill. Push the blunt end of your drill in the stone's hollow and rest the sharp end in the hole on your board. Alternatively, make a hole in a piece of hardwood that fits in your hand and use that instead of the stone.

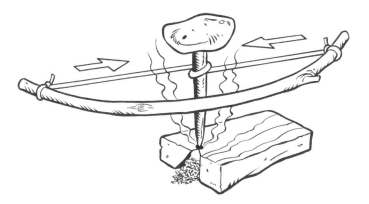

9. Kneel on one knee and place your other foot firmly on the fireboard. Push down lightly on the stone with one hand and hold the bow in your other. Pull the bow back and forth. Begin slowly, and keep a steady pace.

Spin the drill until wood dust and smoke start to come out of the hole.

10. When you see smoke coming out of the hole, push and pull the bow faster and harder. The wood dust will fall into your notch and onto your tinder. When smoke starts to come from your pile of tinder, you have made a "coal." Gently blow on the smoke to produce a flame.

11. Now that you have a little fire, you can add some small sticks, followed by some bigger ones until your flame looks stronger. You can then build your campfire around it using larger pieces of wood.

Survival Tip: Hold your bow horizontally and your drill vertically. A pinch of sand in the hole under the drill will create more friction, and therefore more heat. If there are two of you, take turns with the bow, so that your wood powder doesn't cool down while you are taking a break.

SURVIVAL SKILL WARNINGS:

It is extremely dangerous to start a fire. Always follow the advice below when starting a fire in a survival situation:

• Keep a container of water or soil on hand in case you need to put out your fire quickly.

• Choose a suitable spot for your fire, away from anything that could catch fire, such as trees, bushes, dry grass, and buildings.

• Make sure that all your belongings are out of the way and remove any stones from the area, as they could get really hot and shatter.

• Always keep an eye on the fire to make sure it does not get out of control. When you have finished, make sure you put the fire out and that no embers are left glowing.

HOW TO SURVIVE A FAMILY CHRISTMAS

Forget alien or zombie attacks — studies have shown that there's nothing more alarming than your extended family invading for the Christmas holidays. Here's how to ensure your own survival.

Find out what time your relatives are due to arrive and offer to go shopping for last-minute supplies at that exact moment. This may not be ideal — no one likes shopping — but you will avoid the "meet-and-greet" stage. This is the time when your head is patted, your cheeks are pinched, and you are buried under an avalanche of hairy-chinned kisses and cries of "Look how much you've grown!"

Take advantage of having lots of people in the house and run for cover! In the middle of all the hubbub, you'll find it much easier than usual to slip away unnoticed and have some time to yourself. Hiding behind the Christmas tree is an option, but may be difficult. Instead, take a flashlight, some snacks, and a good book and head for your room. The closet or under the bed make excellent hiding places.

IF ALL ELSE FAILS

Make a plan with your friends to meet up at the movies or to go bowling the day after Christmas. You will need excellent persuasive skills to achieve this, as you will probably have to be excused from a variety of family activities. Siblings who want to tag along can be a particular problem. Think ahead and have a decent bribe ready to keep your brother or sister from pointing out how unfair it is that you get to escape, or from asking to go with you.

Survival Tip: Keep your ears open at all times for any announcements regarding presents. Be sure not to miss out on the best part of the festivities just because you were busy planning your escape.

HOW TO WADE THROUGH RUNNING WATER

Wading through fast-flowing water can be very dangerous. So the rule is never wade unless you absolutely have to. For example, if you are being chased by a water-hating wild animal and you simply can't get around the water, there's no bridge or boat, and you have no way to build a raft, go ahead and wade. But never wade through water that is higher than your knees.

PICK YOUR SPOT

• Make time to look at the stretch of water you're planning to cross, and if there's time, find out as much about it as possible. How deep is it? How fast is the current? Are there any obvious shallows, sandbanks, islands, low overhanging tree branches, or large rocks that might help you cross?

• Choose the best crossing site you can. Look for the area with the shallowest water and the gentlest current. Currents travel faster on the outside of a river bend than on the inside, so avoid outside bends. It is very hard to tell how strong the current is just by looking at the surface of the water. However, the shallower the water, the less force the current will exert on you as you wade. The pressure of fast-flowing water on your legs will come as a shock at first, and it will increase as you edge deeper into the water.

• Look for a stretch of river where the banks are low. That way it will be easier to get in and out of the water.

• Very cold water can be extremely dangerous, as it will affect your body's ability to function. Never attempt to wade through water that is too cold.

OVER AND OUT

1. Make a wading staff. This should be a strong, straight stick, cut to about the height of your shoulder. If possible, make a wrist loop from string or cord and lash it to the staff about 8 inches from the upper end. This will keep the staff from getting lost if you drop it.

2. Take your pants off, but keep your boots on. You will need them to grip the riverbed, and they will protect your feet from anything sharp underwater.

3. Undo the belt of your backpack so that you can remove it quickly if you lose your footing while crossing.

4. Try to keep your belongings dry. Make a raft for your clothes and backpack from a waterproof sheet or tarp. Put a bundle of sticks and some straw in the center of your sheet (to create some air pockets), pile your clothes on top, then tie up the bundle with cord. Attach it to your belt. When the time comes, carefully float the bundle in front of you as you wade across.

5. Use your wading staff to test the riverbed and the depth of the water ahead of you. Even shallow places may have deep potholes, and there are often unseen obstacles such as hidden rocks or waterlogged branches,

or sudden patches of sticky mud or sand. The staff will also help you to keep your balance. If possible, and provided the current allows, use any exposed sandbanks or large rocks as resting places during your crossing.

6. Choose a route that will take you across the river diagonally upstream, to another low bank. Face upstream, in the direction of the oncoming water. Turn your body so that you are inching your feet sideways across the river. Do not take steps as though you are walking. Instead, shuffle your feet underwater, one step at a time, using the staff to help you stay upright.

7. Don't hurry, and don't make any sudden movements. If one boot misses its footing, use your staff and the other foot to recover your balance.

8. If you lose your footing, don't panic. Lie on your back and let the current take you, feet first, downstream, using your hands as paddles to guide you into shallow water where you can stand up again.

SURVIVAL SKILL WARNING:

Wading through water is a skill that should not be used when your street floods. In everyday life, you should never wade through water that is higher than your ankles. Stick to wading through your bathwater. You know how deep it is in there.

HOW TO MAKE A DUGOUT CANOE

One day you stumble across a big fallen tree in your backyard. You and your family can work together to make a dugout canoe from the tree by digging out the wood from the tree trunk. You can demonstrate your amazing survival know-how and test your skill for matching different people to different tasks.

CHOP, CHOP!

1. Cut the branches from the fallen tree. Give this job to a big, strong, adult family member. Then ask that person to saw off the length of trunk that will form your canoe.

2. Next, select someone to remove all the bark from the trunk.

3. When the trunk is bare, look carefully at how it is shaped and decide which end will be the slightly pointy front of the canoe (called the prow). Before turning the trunk over to begin digging out the wood, you will need someone to shape the prow. It needs to form a gentle point that will cut through the water when you are paddling.

4. Next, get all of your family members to work together to gently turn the trunk over. Wedge it firmly to keep it from rolling.

5. Before you begin digging out the interior of the canoe, mark out where the sides will be by scratching some marks in the wood. That way your team will only chop out wood that is inside that mark. If everyone works steadily for several days, the inside of the canoe will begin to appear.

6. Collect the chopped-out wood and put it in a safe place so it can be used as firewood.

7. As the wood is chopped out, the inside surfaces should be carefully shaped and smoothed so the sides are the same thickness all the way around.

Survival Tip: Be careful how your family chops out the wood. If they cut too close to the edge of the tree trunk they could weaken the sides or bottom of your canoe, or worse still, put a hole right through them.

Ask everyone to cut notches across the trunk so that the chunks of wood between them can be chopped out more easily.

Remain patient at all times. Making a dugout canoe will take a long time, but it will all be worth it when you and your family can paddle your canoe down a river.

FINISHING TOUCHES

When work has finished on the inside, roll the canoe over together and finish shaping the outside, chopping away any lumps to cut down the weight of your canoe. Use sandpaper to smooth the surface so it will glide through the water.

The last job is to make the canoe waterproof both inside and out. Some dugout canoe makers use boiled tree resin, which they spread over the wood. However, there are boat-building oils and varnishes that will do the same job and are much easier to use. Waterproof the canoe all over.

Your dad will be itching to try out the canoe on some water as soon as the last waterproof layer is brushed on, but it is up to you to make him wait until the canoe is completely dry, inside and out.

Don't let anyone be too ambitious on the first outing. Instead, plan a short trip in calm waters. Dugout canoes need to be paddled gently.

If the canoe feels a bit wobbly when everyone is inside, you can fit small supports called outriggers on either side. These are hollowed-out lengths of wood that are attached to the canoe by poles. When these are fitted securely, they will balance the canoe and reduce the chance of it tipping over.

Finally, you'll need paddles and flotation devices. Cushions will give members of your family something comfortable to kneel on while they are paddling.

SURVIVAL SKILL WARNING:

Never try to make a dugout canoe by yourself. For one thing it will take you about a year, and for another thing, you run the risk of chopping your fingers instead of chopping the tree trunk. Always make sure you and all of your family members wear flotation devices when you're in your canoe or near the water.

HOW TO BE A MODEST HERO

Display heroic behavior at all times, but always be modest. Remember:

• Actions speak louder than words. Always do your fair share of the really unpopular tasks so that everyone can see you are prepared to pull your weight.

• Give your seat to older people on buses or trains. It shows you are both kind and considerate. Help an old lady safely across the street whenever you can (but only when you're sure she wants to be on the other side).

• No matter how much your arm hurts after falling out of a tree after having saved a kitten from certain death, brush aside offers of help or sympathy. Say things like "It's nothing," or "I'm used to this kind of pain." Cry later when you get home; your mom won't tell anyone. You'll always be a hero to her.

• Never boast. True heroes are quiet and unassuming. Play down all your achievements. If other people want to sing your praises, just shrug or shake your head as if you are embarrassed by the attention.

HOW TO SURVIVE YOUR TEACHERS

School survival skills are among the most important skills you will ever learn.

TEACHER TYPES

There are many types of teachers. Some think they are too cool for school and wear wacky clothes. Others know there is something you would much rather be doing but they give you a mega-impossible project to do, anyway. These are the same teachers who would prefer it if you handed in the work late so that they can tell you off.

TEACHER'S PET

It doesn't matter what your teachers are like, the following tips will keep you in everyone's good book:

• Be on time. This sounds boring, but teachers hate it when you are late and will use it as an excuse to pick on you for the rest of the day. Getting in early means you won't be put on the spot later when you might not have been paying attention.

• Remember the excuses that work. If you hear your teacher shouting at a friend because he or she claimed the dog ate his or her homework, don't use that one yourself (even if your dog really did eat your homework). Make your excuses long and complicated. Hopefully, your teacher will be bored by the time you get to the end, or even better yet, stop you halfway through and just tell you to bring in your homework tomorrow.

• Show some enthusiasm. Teachers find this encouraging and it makes the lesson go much quicker. Ask intelligent questions or request help when you need it. This shows that you want to learn and that you're not just sitting there waiting to go home.

• Everyone gets caught talking in class at some point. If this happens to you, you'll need to think quickly about what you were supposed to have been studying and claim

that you were talking about that. Taking time to look up a relevant subject at the beginning of the class can save you from detention later.

HOMEWORK AVOIDANCE TACTICS

Now it is time for an advanced survival skill — homework avoidance. This should only be attempted if you are confident of success. For best results, pick a Friday afternoon class. Teachers, believe it or not, are as tired of school as you are on Fridays, so they are vulnerable to this prank at this time. About ten minutes before the final bell, put your hand up and ask a question. You must choose this question carefully. It must be relevant to the subject, but require an incredibly long and complicated answer. Here are some examples:

Math: "I read that people didn't always have negative numbers or zero. What did they do before that?"

History: "Do you think that in two thousand years' time they will describe our era as the Middle Ages?"

Your teacher will, if you are lucky, be very impressed by your curiosity and will ramble on answering it until the bell rings, completely forgetting to assign your homework for the weekend.

Survival Tip: Don't overdo it. Putting your hand up first and finding everything your teacher says fascinating will impress your teacher but not your classmates. Always remember you are trying to survive your teacher, not be asked to sit with him or her at lunchtime.

Treat your family to something
AMAZING!

The **Family** *Book*

AMAZING
THINGS TO DO **TOGETHER**

- **OPTICAL ILLUSIONS AND MAGIC TRICKS**
- **MIND-BOGGLING PUZZLES AND RIDDLES**
- **UNIQUE ARTS AND CRAFTS** *And more!*